10 Steps To Creating Self-Discipline

Giovanni Dangel

Table of Contents

Introduction

I want to thank you and congratulate you for downloading the book, *"10 steps to creating Self-Discipline"*

Self-discipline is the ability to face the strongest form of temptation and overcome. Supposing you find yourself in a situation where someone very attractive tries to seduce you when you have made a vow to stay sex-free for a certain period of time, the ability to ignore the seductive moves of that stunningly attractive seducer is self-discipline.

Self-discipline is that ability to cut down on what you live on in order to save more money for more important things. For instance, if you have been living in a duplex all your life and suddenly you decide to become a minimalist, the ability to move from your comfortable duplex to a one bedroom apartment is self-discipline.

Self-discipline is the ability to stay home because you want to study more for your exams and make better grades when your peers are out there partying.

Self-discipline is the ability to quit drinking and smoking by thinking about the health risks you are exposed to as a result of your continued addiction to those harmful drugs and excess alcohol.

It is self-discipline that helps you say no to those MacDonald's fries you have come to love so much to enable you to keep your weight under check. Imagine where you are asked to quit taking your favorite MacDonald's burgher simply because you have put on some weight and would love to shed the unwanted fats. Giving up your favorite things whether food, drink or cloth could be one of the most difficult things in the world. So that ability to give it all up because you desire a better life is self-discipline.

This book deals with all aspects of self-discipline such as what it really is, what causes it, what you lose to lack of it, its benefits, natural ways to build it, and daily habits to sustain and increase it.

Thanks again for downloading this book, I hope you enjoy it!

Are you ready to transform your life and reach your optimal potential?

VISIT:

The Genius Power
unleash the genius within

WWW.THEGENIUSPOWER.COM

Step 1
Know your Self-Control, And Willpower

In order understand the importance of self-discipline, self-control and willpower; we must first define just what these seemingly simple but powerful words mean. Upon doing so, we can then gain a better grasp regarding the factors that could affect the development of these tools and abilities whether in a negative or positive way.

Self-discipline and self-control are actually closely related to one another and the words are often taken to be interchangeable. In particular, self-control entails setting an end goal or reward as a motivation to suppress your emotions, behavior, and innate desire for instant gratification. Self-control can also be sometimes referred to as self-regulation. Meanwhile, self-discipline is the ability to avoid indulging in anything of excess that could lead to future repercussions and negative outcomes. The indulgent behavior that you may wish to exact a certain form of self-control or self-discipline on could be as simple as avoiding dessert after a big meal or as major as submitting an important report before the assigned deadline.

Your self-control and self-discipline could be manifested in any number of ways. They could manifest physically as in your body's endurance and ability to push against the pain and fatigue. They could also manifest mentally, and possibly spiritually as well, as in your mind's ability to exercise restraint in the face of something that is particularly difficult to fight against. Likewise, and possibly most importantly, self-control and self-discipline could manifest in your ability to actually push through and complete your plans even if faced with the greatest adversities.

Willpower is not an ability that you can be born with. It is constantly honed and developed by years of practice. It is a strength that is not physically manifested. Nevertheless, this inner strength is invaluable in helping you make correct and upright decisions and choices in your daily life. It likewise gives you the inner strength to execute tasks that need your immediate attention even despite being surrounded by temptations and natural instincts of instant gratification.

Willpower works hand in hand with self-control and self-discipline in helping you achieve your highest goals. When you learn to develop these three important tools and abilities in yourself, it is akin to having a powerful force that drives you towards your ambitions. You are firmer in your resolve, more determined, and resolute.

The biggest obstacle that could potentially hinder you from utilizing the full capacities of self-control, self-discipline and willpower is a simple, unassuming act called procrastination. If you have found yourself in any situation that you actually delay doing what you intend to do because of either dislike or simple laziness, you are in fact already committing procrastination. If these acts of procrastination are compounded over a period of time they could likely be self-destructive and detrimental to your potential as well as to your career. You could likewise lose the confidence of the people around you since they can no longer trust you to live up to your promises.

You could be a procrastinator and not even know it. The avoidance of a task is not necessarily dependent on gratification of any sort. You could actually be quite convinced in your ability to accomplish tasks and manage your time, but you could still be a procrastinator in other aspects of your life. Therefore, the first step you must take in order to control procrastination is to recognize when you actually start to procrastinate.

After you have figured that out, you can then try to discover the specific reasons for your reaction. These triggers could range from mundane events like answering emails or texts to important events such as when to start applying for graduate school. The reason you could be delaying these tasks is because you simply find them unpleasant or overwhelming to deal with. You could also be otherwise too disorganized to figure out the more essential problems that you should address. Surprisingly, your perfectionism could also be a trigger for your procrastination. You could delay doing a task simply because you find that the conditions are not perfect. By recognizing these reasons, you will be able to take more active steps in order to combat and remedy them and eventually learn to better maximize your time.

Self-control, self-discipline, and willpower will help you to avoid succumbing to procrastination, laziness, and excess in your life and lifestyle. They could provide you with the short term results of becoming more physically active or losing weight if you are used to a sedentary lifestyle. They can likewise help provide you with the long term results of learning to develop more positive habits and a better outlook in life.

Step 2
Stop Procrastination

Procrastination is one of the most common threats to your success. Although you may be organized and confident in your ability to do what you have and want to do, you are still not immune to the effects of procrastination.

Procrastination will prevent you from maximizing your time and ultimately reaching your goals. Therefore, you must learn to hone your tools of self-control, self-discipline, and willpower in order to control procrastination before it becomes an unbreakable habit. There are a few simple steps that you can follow in order to break the cycle and truly discover how much better it is when you impose self-discipline in your life.

The first step is to simply do something instead of delaying it for any trivial reason. Using various forms of delaying tactics will only end up making a bothersome task all the more difficult because of all your wasted time. It is best to just force yourself to get something done as soon as possible instead of waiting for the perfect time and perfect conditions.

The second step is to stop blowing things out of proportion. Often the fear of doing something is worse than actually doing it. The more you dwell on a task and think of how difficult and awful it is, the more it will seem exactly as how you imagine it to be.

Although making a certain strategy to help you tackle a particular project is important, if you spend too much time making a complicated plan for a relatively easy task you will never get anything done. You may try to plan a little at the start and just handle minor problems as you go along. Who knows, you might even realize that the task is not as hard as you thought.

The third step is to take things one step at a time. You should not let the tasks that you have set before you completely overwhelm your mind and scare you from starting anything at all. Tackle each task one at a time and take each task as a step forward toward your goal. Remember to keep your focus on what you have to do today and don't fear the future. You will get to your goal someday, but the important thing right now is the present task.

The fourth step is to tackle the hard problems first before proceeding to the easier tasks. If you have too many thoughts and worries at the back of your mind, your plans could end up being easily derailed. You might also end up searching for a form of escape if you become overwhelmed by the many things you have to do with your limited time. Therefore, it is best to simply handle all of the important things early on. Once you get those tasks out of the way, you will feel less pressure in accomplishing the smaller problems throughout the rest of the day.

The last step is to remember to always finish what you have started. Leaving tasks unfinished is almost as bad as not starting them at all. You will end up feeling stressed and unfulfilled because of the tasks that you will have to carry over to the next day. Since you are already aware of how delaying a task will only make it worse, not finishing a task will cause you similar distress.

Although of course it is discouraged that you rush any project, it is still unwise to leave things unfinished. It is, therefore, best that you use your self-discipline to motivate you to simply do as much as you can without rushing until you finally successfully finish your task. The satisfaction that you get from a job well done is what will ultimately motivate you to fight the urge to procrastinate in the future.

Step 3
Daily Habits to Increase Your Level of self-discipline

It is not just about developing or building self-discipline, it is also important to ensure that you sustain and increase your self-discipline by engaging in some daily activities that make you more disciplined. Here are some daily habits you could cultivate to improve your level of self-discipline.

1. Have an Attitude of Gratitude

Don't spend your whole life thinking of things you would have loved to have, which for one reason or the other have eluded you thus far. Having an attitude of gratitude teaches you to be thankful for what you have. Having an attitude of gratitude for the little you have can open the doors for the plenty you desire to flood into your life. This attitude of gratitude even when you obviously do not have enough helps you build your self-discipline.

Gratitude comes with a whole lot of benefits. From improving the state of your mental health to enhancing your emotional wellbeing. Most importantly, gratitude helps you detach from your state of lack and scarcity. Thinking about the things you desire which you have not been able to get will make it hard for you to attain the level of self-discipline you need to achieve your goals.

2. Forgive

When it comes to forgiveness, you must learn to forgive both yourself and others to enable you to get ahead in life. Learning to forgive yourself when you err and others when they hurt you helps build up your energy for success and makes you more disciplined. Whenever people hurt you, just forgive them and empty your mind of a load of hate and malice. Forgiving people who hurt you helps you release every negative energy that makes you lose your self-discipline.

3. Set Active Goals For Each Day

Active goals are active because they can be seen. You make your goals active by putting them down on paper and placing them where they can be seen. Active goals help you build and increase your level of self-discipline because they give your life daily directions.

4. Eat Right

When you eat the right foods, you help your body store more energy. When your diet is mostly composed of fats, carbohydrates, and proteins, your body dissipates lots of energy processing such foods. When you eat more of fruits and veggies which require less energy to be processed, you will experience an energy boost that will help you pursue your goals with an adequate level of self-discipline.

5. Get Enough Sleep

There is a direct link between sleep and self-discipline. Whether you give your body enough rest by getting adequate sleep or not goes a long way to determining your ability to stay focused on your goal to achieve self-discipline and your general well-being. Make sure you get 6-8 hours of sleep no matter how busy you are. Avoid caffeinated drinks before bedtime.

6. Exercise Daily

Incorporating physical exercises into your daily routines helps you get rid of bad habits and adopt positive habits. If you really want to learn to discipline yourself, make certain physical exercises part of your morning routine. Most people give the excuse that they are too busy or have a lot of worries to get involved in physical exercises. Where such people get it wrong is that they forget they can improve their entire lives through physical exercises. Engaging in daily exercises helps you get rid of pains, anxiety, stress, and fatigue because when you exercise, your body releases hormones like endorphin and neurotransmitters such as serotonin and dopamine.

7. Stay organized

Don't just wake up and start working on your goals for the day. Make sure you have your goals and daily tasks arranged in an orderly manner. Arranging your goals in an orderly manner helps you stay organized which is a good sign of self-discipline. Being organized goes beyond having a list of things to do in their order or priorities. It also involves organizing all areas of your life such as your work table, your drawer, your kitchen cabinets, your wardrobe, your garage, your bedroom, and all other such spaces in your life.

Step 4
Meditation techniques to Increase Self Discipline

For some people, particularly those with type A personalities, meditation can seem like a wasteful, boring task. However, if you actually take the time to meditate even for a few minutes each day, you will be surprised at just how much your meditation sessions can impact the way you do things and the way you accomplish simple tasks on a daily basis. The changes will indeed be gradual and not particularly noticeable for other people. Nevertheless, you will easily be able to detect the changes that are happening to yourself. You will be able to see how meditation will be able to improve your focus, energy, and confidence. Most importantly, you will see how meditation can help you improve and increase your self-discipline.

Meditation strategies are can come in a number of forms and there are in fact so many types of meditation strategies that you can try out. You can try Yoga meditation, creative visualization, Buddhist meditation, Christian meditation, Hindu meditation, and much more.

You can choose to try any one or any combination of these strategies to see which will best suit your lifestyle and needs. There is no right or wrong meditation strategy. The most important thing is that you find the optimal meditation strategy that you are most compatible with. That particular meditation strategy will give you the most benefit and the best results. However, if you become overwhelmed with all of the various meditation strategies available to you, you can simply make your own meditation style. You can break down the strategies to their basic components and customize them according to your needs.

It is important to note that at the core of each individual meditation strategy is a focus. This focus could range from a physical object to mental concepts. You could select your point of focus to range from a tangible object to a prayer or mantra. Although it is inevitable for your thoughts to wander during those moments of silence, having a point of focus will help your remain mindful and more self-aware.

Simple breathing exercises can in fact already help you learn to be more mindful. You will be required to pay attention to the sound of your breath and heartbeat and notice the way your chest rises and falls. This simple act not only relaxes your mind and improves your blood flow, it also helps you be more focused on the impact that every single act has on yourself. If you become aware of the things you do, you will have more self-control to avoid committing careless mistakes and indulging in potentially destructive impulses.

After you have found your focus, the second part would be developing your meditation warm-up strategy. Similar to how a proper warm up will prepare you for strenuous physical exercise, a meditation warm up strategy will also prepare you for serious concentration. Your warm up strategy may begin with your physical body and slowly progress to your emotional and mental consciousness. An example would be starting with basic stretching and later moving on to your controlled breathing technique until you find your inner peace and energy.

Time for introspection is the general objective of meditation. Introspection will allow you to become more self-aware and mindful of your strengths and weaknesses. You can more easily find the aspects and specific areas in yourself that you need to improve on. Eventually, meditation will motivate you to exercise more conscious control over your life. You will be better able to decide on the changes that you want to see and the concrete actions that you should take in order to set those things in motion.

The last core component in meditation is the integration process. This process essentially aims to assimilate your meditation activity as an important part of your daily routine. The more often you meditate, the more likely it is that it will become a daily habit.

You can initiate the integration process by setting a specific time within the day that you will be required to meditate. The most convenient time would usually be the first few minutes after waking. It will be easier for you to set time for meditation if you have a schedule to follow. Consistently following the schedule will not only ensure that meditation becomes a daily habit. It is also in fact already a way to practice and hone your self-discipline.

Meditation will provide you with the needed mental skill of complete focus. The ability to focus will help to increase your self-discipline and enable you to rise above the influence of external and internal distractions and temptations. You will learn to be more decisive in the choices that you make because you are confident that you made those choices using your self-awareness and your self-control. As a result, you will be able to have more peace of mind and feel more satisfied with your life.

Step 5
Train Your Brain to take The Right Decision

Although you might think that it is impossible to make the right decision in every possible situation, it is indeed possible as long as you avoid succumbing to your fatal flaw of human irrationality. You are actually already equipped with the necessary tools to make good decisions. You simply need to use your self-discipline to overcome the temptations of distractions that could prevent you from reaching your goal.

Keeping your thoughts in a rational state helps you take into account all possible outcomes that could result from a decision and confidently weigh their respective pros and cons. You already have this capability to easily organize your thoughts, but if you do not have enough willpower to resist sudden temptations then you can be still easily distracted. You must train yourself to keep your eye on the prize and, if necessary, periodically remind yourself in order to keep your focus.

You will also have to remember that every decision you make will eventually not only affect your life but the lives of many others. This will help you give more importance to every choice you make and motivate you to make the right decision every time. However, it is important that you do not let yourself be overwhelmed by the gravity of your choice and let that fear possibly prevent you from taking action. You should simply learn to take a calculated risk and rely on your good sense that you have made the best decision for the benefit of the majority.

Sometimes, it is also best to simply take a breather and stop overthinking and over analyzing things. It is possible that you may need to stop using your brain and start using your intuition or gut feeling to help you arrive at the right choice.

It could be that you already know what you want or what you need but you just don't find that thing possible or acceptable at the moment. The passage of time will change things and what you had once considered unacceptable then could already be a possibility in the present. Once you learn to simply go with the flow, it is more likely that you will find it much easier to figure out the steps needed to set your plans in motion.

In the end, although your brain can help you think things through and help you carefully plan your actions, it can be easily overwhelmed by copious amounts of conflicting information. This makes your brain prone to irrational thoughts that could lead you to make wrong and potentially damaging decisions.

During certain times that you find yourself overwhelmed by the repercussions a certain decision may have, it is best that you find a way to quiet your mind and instead listen to your intuition. That intuitive feeling is of course not meant to be taken at face value. It is instead meant to facilitate your decision making by pointing you in the right direction. Acknowledging your gut feel will help you eliminate most of the wrong paths that you are contemplating to take. Combining rational thought and intuition is guaranteed to make it easier for you to come to the right decision every time.

Step 6
Know your Bad Decision Making and Loss of Self Control

Making decisions, preferably good decisions, is in essence a very simple act. All that you are required to do is to set a specific goal that you want to achieve and weigh that against the actual value of achieving it. Afterwards you just need to weigh all of your possible options and choose the one that will give you the best possible outcome. However, this rational process just cannot be perfectly executed by the human mind. As much as we try to deny it, humans are simply prone to committing irrational acts and decisions. These bad decisions form an endless cycle of regret and ultimately the greater the number of bad decisions you have made in the past, the more decisions you are likely to make in the future.

Your past bad decisions that have resulted in giving you regret have likewise given you a sense of fear in committing even more bad decisions. However despite this fear you are still unable to make a rational choice especially when higher stakes are involved. In case you are presented with a situation that could either result in huge losses or huge gains, your brain will be pressured to make the choice that will cause the least amount of regret in the long run. Unfortunately, these choices, though safe, may not necessarily be the right choices to make. You could end up putting more value on not messing up too badly and ending up with regret that you lose sight of the actual goal that you had intended to achieve in the first place.

Past memories of regret are often harder to forget than past memories that contain average feelings. The reason for this is that regret instills a certain kind of pain that stays with you every time you look back on your past mistakes. These past decisions could adversely influence both your present and your future decisions if they are allowed to cloud your judgment. The sting of the memory of a bad experience could make you disregard all of the other present and future options that you were actually hoping to weigh in order to come to the best decision. Your irrational thinking will make you choose the outcome according to how things could have possibly turned up in the past. You will therefore end up disregarding the rational thought that you are at a different time now and are most likely dealing with different stakes.

The passage of time is apparently not enough to guarantee growth and maturity when it comes to making decisions during stressful situations. It may be hard to do in the beginning, but you will have to learn to stop relying on past actions and mistakes. You must instead learn to focus on current as well as on future possibilities in order to break out of the otherwise endless cycle of bad decisions.

Self-control, or more specifically the loss of self-control, also plays an important role in influencing your decisions. Loss of self-control could result from your innate need for instant gratification. However because you can become so focused on immediately getting that pleasurable feeling, you may end up disregarding the other long term consequences of your actions. That instant gratification could in fact come at the expense of other options that you should have considered. In effect, you end up with a bad decision.

Sometimes as well, even when you try to make a good decision, you just might not have access to the right information. You could also be otherwise presented with an overwhelming amount of information. This could compromise your ability to separate the unnecessary information from the information necessary in aiding you to make the right decision. When you become unable to find the necessary information, you could end up being easily swayed by the simple opinions of the other people close to you. You could end up putting more weight on their biases and end up disregarding all of the available information completely.

In order to avoid succumbing to the biased opinions of others, you must make a conscious effort to take their words with a grain of salt. Their circumstances and lives are decidedly different from yours, and their opinions were formed as a result of their particular experiences. Therefore, what works for them might not necessarily work for you. In the end, it is ultimately better to make your decisions by weighing the different sources of reliable information and using those to come at the best informed decision.

In the end, even when you are faced with all of these unfavorable issues, it is still actually possible to make the right decisions. You just have to be self-aware and have self-control over your own irrational thinking. Once you realize that you are relying on your emotional impulses instead of your rational impulses, you have to exercise your self-control and stop for a while and calm yourself down. You have to recalibrate your thoughts to focus only on your major goal and not allow yourself to be so easily distracted by other external factors. Although it might take some time before you are able to master this technique, it will end up being an extremely beneficial ability that you can use to improve many aspects of your life.

Step 7 some Techniques to Increase Self Discipline

In order to break out of the cycle of constant disorder and self-disappointment, you will have to learn to take your life in your own hands. You deserve a life where you are not at constant war with yourself and your desires. Therefore, you will need to take concrete steps that will lead you gain more willpower and self-discipline so that you can become motivated to achieve your full potential. If you have enough willpower, you can essentially simply set a goal and successfully make that a reality.

Exercising willpower and self-discipline can be likened to exercising a muscle in the human body. Although constant and excessive use could lead to fatigue, long term use could likewise lead to increased strength and mastery. If these skills are constantly used in practical application over a consistent period of time, it is more likely that you will find it easier to use the skills in any situation that you need them.

In the same way that proper exercise techniques could help strengthen your physical body, certain techniques can also be used to strengthen your mental willpower and self-discipline. Consistently practicing self-discipline on smaller tasks first could better strengthen your resolve and willpower to accomplish much larger tasks in the future.

The first technique that you can utilize is to eliminate possible temptations from your life is to avoid all temptations. Since overuse of your willpower and self-discipline could lead fatigue or burnout, you will have to learn to conserve your available reserves of strength. In order to maximize the willpower that you do possess, you will have to choose the situations that you should actually be involved in. This entails that you be conscious of the possible circumstances that could tempt you to procrastinate or otherwise cause you to overindulge. It is best that you conserve your willpower so that you will still have enough reserve self-control to face emergencies and make important decisions when the time arises.

One simple example would be avoiding walking in areas where there are a lot of fast food establishments that could tempt you particularly if you are on a diet. Another would be keeping televisions, computers, and possibly even radios turned off when you are studying for important exams or writing reports in order to avoid the unnecessary distractions. These simple steps of prevention could already help you in finding it easier to determine and avoid the sources of temptation that cause you to use up too much of your willpower.

Another technique you should apply in order to increase your will power is to simply get adequate sleep and eat enough healthy food. When your body is in a state of instability as a result of poor food choices and poor sleeping habits, your decision making skills can be compromised. Likewise, your self-discipline could be diminished. Your body is craving for too many things at once thus affecting your ability to focus on any one important task. You may also succumb much easier to the lure of instant gratification.

Unsurprisingly, reducing stress and enjoying life more can motivate you to practice your willpower. Those simple moments of happiness could hopefully be enough to encourage you to think more positively. They could also help you realize the direct benefit of exercising self-discipline on your lifestyle. You will be able to understand that the more you practice yourself discipline and accomplish important tasks, the more time you will have to expend for recreational activities.

Planning for both short-term goals and long-term goals could help you improve your willpower. Possibly writing down those goals and placing them at an easily visible area can also provide you with the tangible inspiration you need in order to keep your focus. You will be further motivated to work towards your goal since you can already physically track your progress.

You can easily practice your willpower to complete tasks at the time that they present themselves in order to avoid falling into the trap of procrastination. You will no longer wait for the most convenient time to accomplish your tasks since every item crossed out from your list is enough to motivate you. Eventually making plans and tracking your progress will become second nature and you will actually look forward to making those lists that give structure to your life.

Lastly, the best technique you can use to strengthen your self-discipline is to set up a reward system for yourself for every time that you successfully utilize your willpower to accomplish your tasks. These rewards can serve as short-term goals that help motivate you to persevere and achieve even more. They can likewise help make the process of working towards a long term goal much more enjoyable.

Starting out is always the hardest part in every undertaking. This is particularly true if you have been accustomed to an unstructured and undisciplined lifestyle. However if you want to get anywhere, you must choose to take your life into your own hands right this minute. These techniques will help to strengthen your willpower and self-discipline so that you will no longer be intimidated to attempt to achieve long term goals in the future. Ultimately, in order to achieve any goal, you will actually have to believe that you have the strength and self-discipline to capably do whatever you set your mind to.

Step 8 How to Use your NLP to Increase Self Control

Neuro-linguistic programming or NLP is a form of psychotherapy that was developed by Richard Bandler and John Grinder in the 1970s. The NLP techniques are said to utilize the connection between language, behavioral patterns, and the brain's neurological processes in order to achieve specific goals. NLP basically uses the power of suggestion to help you possibly change the way you remember and think about certain things and events. Hypnotherapy often utilizes NLP in order to cure people of their phobias, behavioral disorders, etc.

Learning NLP techniques could help you to increase your self-control and will power. NLP aims to help you gain more focus and control thereby increasing your self-discipline in the process. Once you already have a clear goal in mind, you will find it easier to utilize your willpower to get the job done.

The benefits of practicing NLP are meant to not only increase your self-discipline but to likewise increase your confidence and help you eliminate your bad work and life habits. In order to accomplish those things, you will have to learn a few NLP techniques and consistently apply them in your daily life.

The first and most popular NLP technique that you can use to increase your self-discipline is called anchoring. The anchor in this method is not something that will hold you down, rather it is something that will ground you and help you keep your focus. Anchoring is akin to setting a certain trigger that will instantly put you in your desired state of mind. The right state of mind will help you to efficiently utilize your willpower to perform any necessary tasks and solve any pending problems.

Another NLP technique that you can use to help you increase your self-discipline is called logical levels. Logical levels will help you better organize the tasks that you need to accomplish in order to reach your goals. This technique will let you utilize your willpower to overcome those periods of overwhelming frustration that could otherwise stall your progress.

The final NLP technique that you can use is called sub modalities. Sub modalities are simply the way your brain interprets certain past, present, and future experiences. It is possible to change the way an experience affects you simply by changing the sub modalities that you associate with that certain experience.

In certain cases where your past mistakes hinder you from making good decisions in the present or future, applying this technique can help you overcome that fear. Changing the feelings that you associate with that event can help lessen its overall impact on your psyche. Your willpower can then help you push through and guide you in making a good decision.

In the end, it is still up to your personal judgment whether you believe that these techniques can help you concretely increase your self-discipline. However, there really is nothing to lose even if you do try them out. In fact, these neuro-linguistic programming techniques could possibly help you improve not only the way you think but even improve the way that you do things.

Step 9 Good Decision Making Habits Using Self Control

In order to consistently make good decisions throughout the day, you must remember to properly utilize your self-control and always consider all of your possible options first before making the best choice. However, this is not always a straightforward and easy task especially for someone who has to constantly make decisions and settle conflicts for long periods. Willpower is not an infinite resource. Spending too much strength all at once could weaken your self-control and lead you to making bad decisions.

The good news is that there exist a few simple rules in good decision making. You can easily conserve the available resource of willpower that you do have if you simply remember to follow these steps.

The first rule that you should remember is that you should not be easily swayed by the biases of others regardless if they are the majority. You should be the leader of your life and the leader of your own self. You possess your own self-control to enable you to utilize your willpower to make well informed decisions.

You may choose to consider the opinions of others as your possible options, but ultimately you have to choose the option that you believe to be the best and most beneficial in the long run.

The best solution could be the most simple and obvious choice, but it may not always be easy to make. That is the reason why you need to exercise your self-control to help you choose the difficult but ultimately the best possible choice.

The second rule that you should remember is that you should be decisive. You should have confidence in your own capability to weigh your options and achieve your goals successfully. You must stand by what you choose and not let past failures bring down your resolve.

The most important thing is that you move on from those past failures and actually learn from them. You should utilize you willpower to block out the negative memories from the past and learn to take more risks. Don't let past fears and failures hinder you from making present and future decisions. Always keep a level head and use your self-control to remain rational even when making the right choice is a complicated task.

It is vital that you actually move forward and make a decision now rather than delay it. Procrastination is the number one cause of bad decision making. Ultimately, the fear that you have in doing something is oftentimes much worse than the actual process of simply getting it done. Utilize your self-control to overcome the procrastination before it becomes a habit that hinders you from making the right decision.

The third rule that you should follow in order to make good decisions is to tackle problems one at a time. Making a list can help you better organize and manage the tasks that you have settle or handle whether for the short term or for the long term. The important thing is to decide which the most important tasks at hand are.

Truthfully, simply choosing the tasks that you will first accomplish will already require utilizing your self-control. You must use your self-control to fight the urge to get the easier but less urgent tasks done first. However, as constantly using your willpower will eventually deplete it, it is best to handle the important tasks one at a time. If you become overwhelmed by the things that you have to handle, you could be more prone to make bad decisions.

Finally, the last rule that you should follow is actually carrying out your decision. Once you have made your choice you will have to follow it through. It is truly no easy task to come to a decision, but the process of problem solving should never end there. You should not feel complacent or comfortable after that first good choice has been made. Successfully solving your problems will require you to take further steps that will require using you willpower and self-control.

Problem solving essentially has two phases. Both of those phases require you to make good decisions. The first phase involves choosing what needs to be done and involves making use of the first three rules in coming up with that good decision. The second phase involves choosing when that first good choice needs to be done. The second phase will essentially set the deadline for determining if the choice you made is truly the best possible choice. A good choice can only be proven to be a good choice if you have existing evidence to back it up. Take concrete steps to actually set your choice in motion in order to ensure that the choice you made will result in the outcome that you want.

Another importance of setting a deadline is that you will still have the opportunity to change your decision if you do not get your desired outcome at the first try. You will have ample time to correct your mistakes and learn from them if you set your plans in motion as soon as possible. Getting your desired outcome will not only give you positive reinforcement, but it will also strengthen your resolve to utilize more of your willpower in making good future decisions.

Step 10
How to use your New Self Discipline Habits to Increase Your Productivity and Maximize Your Potential

It is not just about developing or building self-discipline, it is also important to ensure that you sustain and increase your self-discipline by engaging in some daily activities that make you more disciplined. Here are some daily habits you could cultivate to improve your level of self-discipline.

1. Have an Attitude of Gratitude

Don't spend your whole life thinking of things you would have loved to have, which for one reason or the other have eluded you thus far. Having an attitude of gratitude teaches you to be thankful for what you have. Having an attitude of gratitude for the little you have can open the doors for the plenty you desire to flood into your life. This attitude of gratitude even when you obviously do not have enough helps you build your self-discipline.

Gratitude comes with a whole lot of benefits. From improving the state of your mental health, to enhancing your emotional wellbeing. Most importantly, gratitude helps you detach from your state of lack and scarcity. Thinking about the things you desire which you have not been able to get will make it hard for you to attain the level of self-discipline you need to achieve your goals.

2. Forgive

When it comes to forgiveness, you must learn to forgive both yourself and others to enable you get ahead in life. Learning to forgive yourself when you err and others when they hurt you helps build up your energy for success and makes you more disciplined. Whenever people hurt you, just forgive them and empty your mind of the load of hate and malice. Forgiving people who hurt you helps you release every negative energy that makes you lose your self-discipline.

3. Meditation

Engaging in meditations helps put your mind at ease. It creates a type of spiritual atmosphere around you to help you grow and become a better you. Meditation sets the stage for you to attain a higher state of self-discipline by clearing the palette of your mind and putting you in the right mood to face the challenges of the day.

A simple meditation technique is to sit down on the floor with your legs folded in front of you, close your eyes, remove your mind from all worries, and focus on your breaths with your palms facing upwards.

4. Set Active Goals For Each Day

Active goals are active because they can be seen. You make your goals active by putting them down on paper and placing them where they can be seen. Active goals help you build and increase your level of self-discipline because they give your life daily directions.

5. Eat Right

When you eat the right foods, you help your body store more energy. When your diet is mostly composed of fats, carbohydrates and proteins, your body dissipates lots of energy processing such foods. When you eat more of fruits and veggies which require less energy to be processed, you will experience an energy boost that will help you pursue your goals with adequate level of self-discipline.

6. Get Enough Sleep

There is a direct link between sleep and self-discipline. Whether you give your body enough rest by getting adequate sleep or not goes a long way to determine your ability to stay focused on your goal to achieve self-discipline, and your general well-being. Make sure you get 6-8 hours of sleep no matter how busy you are. Avoid caffeinated drinks before bedtime.

7. Exercise Daily

Incorporating physical exercises into your daily routines helps you get rid of bad habits and adopt positive habits. If you really want to learn to discipline yourself, make certain physical exercises part of your morning routine. Most people give the excuse that they are too busy or have a lot of worries to get involved in physical exercises. Where such people get it wrong is that they forget they can improve their entire lives through physical exercises. Engaging in daily exercises helps you get rid of pains, anxiety, stress, and fatigue because when you exercise, your body releases hormones like endorphin and neurotransmitters such as serotonin and dopamine.

8. Stay organized

Don't just wake up and start working on your goals for the day. Make sure you have your goals and daily tasks arranged in an orderly manner. Arranging your goals in an orderly manner helps you stay organized which is a good sign of self-discipline. Being organized goes beyond having a list of things to do in their order or priorities. It also involves organizing all areas of your life such as your work table, your drawer, your kitchen cabinets, your wardrobe, your garage, your bedroom, and all other such spaces in your life.

Conclusion

Thank you again for downloading this book!

The important role self-discipline plays in your life goes a long way to justify every effort and time you put into building your self-discipline. The techniques outlined in this book will guide you on this self-discipline journey to enable you to live a better and a more meaningful life.

Finally, if you enjoyed this book, then I'd like to ask you for a favor, would you be kind enough to leave a review for this book on Amazon? It'd be greatly appreciated!

Click here to leave a review for this book on Amazon!

Thank you and good luck!